KhanSquash Tips

by

Sakhi Khan

Introduction

These squash tips are an accumulation of my experience as a competitive squash player.

It began at the Harvard Club of Boston at the age of eleven to the present. In that time I was ranked number one in the United States as a junior; competed in college as a four-time All-American varsity player; Represented the USA in the Pan Am games; Won the Massachusetts State Championship; competed in the World Professional Circuit for seven years and finished as a seventeen year college coach up till 2018.

Lastly, I am the fourth generation of the Khan Dynasty squash where for us the game of squash has been in our blood from the earliest recorded championships to the present.

I hope you enjoy reading these tips and I wish you the best of luck in the ultimate mind/body sport of squash.

#1

Smooth movement in a squash court in essential for winning squash. Keep in mind that not only is the correct foot needed, but how you take that crucial step.

Everyone should know a forehand shot is off a left foot and a backhand shot is off a right foot. But, did you know that most players place their feet incorrectly.

What does that mean?

Let's say your opponent hits a crosscourt from the right-hand serve box area to the left-hand serve box area. You anticipate the shot and move towards the ball, striking a backhand off your right foot. Perfect! Is this all that's needed? The answer is no. This is because for most of us anticipation and correct footwork is not enough to speed us up. There is an ingredient missing.

When you twist to step towards a shot, never let your knee rise too high off the ground. Learn to skim the surface, without touching it, with the bottom of your sneakers. Many shots have passed me until I discovered that I didn't need to raise my knee, but that I needed to keep my feet as close to the ground as possible as I ran. This eliminated the hang time created by high stepping to balls.

With your feet closer to the ground as you move, you'll discover that running this way will get you less fatigued and get you to the ball faster, especially for those hard passing shots.

#2

It's time to power up. To hit harder is efficient use of the wrist. Keep the grip on your racquet as thin as possible to give your wrist the flexibility it needs in hard shots.

Keep your elbow in and snap your wrist when the ball is rising. If you start striking the ball on the rise rather than the peak of the bounce, you will snap your wrist faster.

Remember to tighten your grip at the point of impact and not sooner. A hard shot has a uniquely solid feel to it.

It's called the sweet spot. Find it.

#3

The point starts with a serve; it continues into a rally for position; and then either you or your opponent finishes the point with a winner or a mistake. Let's discuss how you should start a point.

The point starts with a serve. This makes the serve important, but many squash players focus on the wrong aspect of the serve. I have seen players try to get their serves tighter and tighter. But, you should know that developing an ace serve is a waste of time. A good serve should be hit close to the walls to restrict your opponent's swing. That is all. Nowhere will you find that you need to develop a service ace. You should concentrate more on your opponent's return. You need to differentiate a rail return from a crosscourt or a drop. What I'm getting at is that, squash serves don't count as much as reading your opponent's return of serve and the way you prepare for the return.

The best way to prepare for a service return is to get in the crouch position. Get ready to pounce on the ball. Make sure your opponent sees this. It'll add mental pressure to his or her return. Mental pressure works best when your opponent sees you hovering on the "T" in the crouch position right after a tight serve. Try it!

#4

All professionals say, "Watch the ball". But, did you know that there is a certain way of watching the ball. During a rally your opponent will be either in front, behind, or parallel to you. There is only one way to watch in each of these circumstances.

When your opponent is in front of you, it is easy to see where and when your opponent is going to hit the ball. The secret is to stay as close to your opponent as possible, without crowding, as he or she is striking the ball. This adds mental pressure onto your opponent because by doing this your opponent knows you're ready, especially for a drop. If your opponent is in front, remember the drop is the most likely shot to be executed. And this means trouble. So get close to your opponent when he or she is in front of you.

When your opponent is next to you or behind you, try not to look directly at the ball. Use your peripheral vision. The reason to do this is that it may be physically impossible to follow a fast crosscourt and turn your head at the same time. Use your eyeballs instead of your head and neck.

A good reference point is the serve line that runs across the court. Follow the ball with your eye to this line and then lock your eye at the serve line area and let your peripheral vision track the ball to your opponent's racquet.

The only exception is if you've hit a high length shot that comes off high on the back wall. In this instance you need to watch your opponent closely. Just make sure you're watching from the front while on the "T".

#5

Everyone improves at different rates, and everyone ends up at different levels. Furthermore, a high standard player today will undoubtedly become a lower standard player tomorrow. No matter where you are in squash, either on the rise or on the fall of your game, you will develop one thing - and that's "experience". An experienced squash player passes through three phases.

The first phase of an experienced squash player is learning to keep the ball in play. Retrieving is good. Stroking is good. Even movement is good. But, everything is done at one standard pace you've chosen that best suits your game plan. This is fine. Everyone usually says you're steady and that you're consistent.

The second phase of an experienced squash player is learning to stay consistent with all the qualities above yet also having the ability to mix the pace. A player can now speed the rally up and slow it down with the effective use of drops and lobs and boasts. This is great. Everyone usually says you're tough to beat.

The third phase of an experienced squash player is a zone only a few can really enter. In this phase the squash player has all the characteristics above with an uncanny intuitive ability to fake. This player draws you in for a rail and hits a boast. He or she can wind up and appear to crush a shot when at the last second changes it into a crosscourt drop.

Where do you stand?

#6

What will make you faster and increase you're winners instantly? What is the one thing that keeps your concentration focused and keeps your opponent from attacking? What do the best squash players possess? It's all in one unique way of playing. Start playing squash by keeping your BALANCE at all times.

Run balanced! Never run into walls! Try to feel your weight balanced under each step and when you slow to strike, keep your balance! Strike the ball from the beginning of your stroke to the end of your stroke without losing your balance! Hover on the T in a crouched balanced position. From here on in focus on how well you're able to stay balanced throughout rallies. Note where and when your balance is lost. Is it on drops? Is it on serve returns? Or is it in the back corners? When you twist do you lose your balance?

Note every spot on the court you seem to lose your balance and start remedying each one. Before you know it, you'll increase your speed and shooting ability just because you paid attention to how

well you're able to stay BALANCED.

7

Squash is a sport requiring stamina. Every squash player realizes this fact as soon as rallies get a bit longer. Many top players train outside the court. Some of them run. Others swim. But, did you know that the top players realize one thing before starting to train outside the squash court. They realize that there are two types of stamina in squash.

Cardiovascular fitness is described above. But, striking the ball with consistency is by far much more crucial. And the pros know this. What I mean is that your arm needs the strength and endurance to hit the ball continuously for an hour with good control. If this is unattainable as of yet, don't waste your time training outside the court until your arm can endure an hour of hard hitting. The pros know that without ball control – you're dead on the tour no matter how fit you are!

Have you noticed how much work your arm does as compared to your legs? If your arm goes, your legs can help you retrieve a bit longer before losing. If your legs go, your arm can still hit winners because you don't need to run for every single shot. But you do need to hit every single shot with your arm. So practice hitting the ball as hard as possible without injuring yourself and see how long you can do it. Keep in mind that you're not just blindly hitting the ball hard. Try to control a twenty shot rail drill and then crosscourt to the other side for another twenty shot rail drill. Keep the ball moving at a high rate. Hit boasts, crosscourts and rails and go for the nick. Watch the ball! Have you ever really watched the ball for an hour without interruption? It's not easy until you try it. Feel the lactic acid build up in your arm.

Before you know it, you'll sense an improvement in your endurance and in your ability to concentrate on watching the ball. Time yourself! Lengthen every practice session by five minutes until you're able to hit relatively hard for a solid hour without let up. After you've achieved this, do what the pros do. Start training outside the court.

#8

One of the main reasons why squash players stop improving is when they start getting into the same routine.

Let's assume you have two or three regular games with the same players every week. Let's also assume you play at the same times and on the same courts. This adds up to the same routine.

Here's a new regiment to consider.

Keep your regular games in your schedule. Just cut down on the frequency. Play the same players you've been accustomed to every other week instead of every week. Use your regulars as reference points to gage your improvement. But, let's start making room for new players.

The best way to meet new players is through tournaments and club leagues in your area. Get involved in these types of squash competitions. The club league matches will expose you to new players that have different tactics. These new tactical strategies to beat you on courts you never played on can be quite a challenge. Anticipating shots and adapting to new styles of play help you focus on your game. If you ever have a great match with a new player, exchange phone numbers for more games at his or her club in the future. In essence, pulling yourself out of your comfort zone will restart your improvement curve.

Try to have matches on different courts. Every court is different. A presumed killer crosscourt may not be as effective on a slower less predictable court. This will resort you to use other shots and probably force you to use a different game plan.

This is what you need to stay on top of your game.

Also, plan a morning match once a week. Playing squash at the same time tends to make you play your best game at that time. Sometime tournament matches are early in the morning, so play a 6am match once a week.

Consider this new regiment. Start looking for new players and different courts to play squash. Use your regular games as reference points and start playing once a week in the morning. This is a great way to kick-start your squash game.

#9

Holding the racquet correctly is very important in squash. But, did you know that the speed of your wrist and power can be enhanced with a slight adjustment to your grip.

The standard grip says to hold the racquet at an angle as if shaking someone's hand. It also says to hold the middle of the grip. Combining both keeps your swing steady.

But, sometimes a fast wrist is needed for a quick kill or a quick reflex shot; and sometimes a player needs that extra power to drive the ball deep into the corners. If you've ever fallen into this sort of a situation, which I'm sure all of you have, then a little grip adjustment could give you an edge.

If you hold the grip up high or choke up, you'll notice a faster wrist immediately. Consider the practice of making contact with the ball with adjustments to your grip. Hit a few shots in the middle grip position, and then hold the grip higher. You'll notice a faster and lighter racquet head. This is ideal for a quick volley and digging out those hard to get deep back wall shots. The higher grip shortens your swing radius helping to make your wrist roll through a shot more comfortably. The more comfortable your wrist, the faster you'll snap it. Use the high grip for all tight shots from the back corners to delicate drops. For drops a quick wrist isn't needed, but the higher grip helps your racquet handling to hit the winner.

Keep practicing alone and now hit the ball while holding the end of the grip. You'll notice a shift in weight to the head of the racquet. This will increase power. I always slide my hand down to the end of the racquet for that crushing power sometimes needed. But, since the racquet feels heavier, I use it when I have time to take a full swing at the ball.

If you practice adjusting your grip, it'll become subconscious during match play. The best titanium or graphite racquets will never improve your wrist or power game unless you know how to do it yourself.

#10

The best athletes know that the fine line between good and great is self-preparation. Self-preparation is preparing your mental state as well as your physical state for peak performance. To be the best player you can be at whatever level you're currently competing at, you need to focus on what makes you play at your best. You need to experiment with foods to see what gives you a boost. You need to discover how many hours of sleep help your performance. In short, you need to know what things to do and not to do before a match. Everyone is different, but I'll give you some suggestions.

I won't go into practicing and training techniques. I will take for granted that you play at least three times a week, swimming or jog twice a week and have a stretching routine. In this tip I'd like to focus on getting ready to play a big match.

Preparing for a match should start the day before. This is the ideal time to carbo load at dinner. I like pasta and Gatorade, but speak with a nutritionist to see what best fits your diet. Also, make sure you get plenty of sleep. Sleep with the thoughts of playing great the next day.

Have a light breakfast and/or lunch. Start thinking about your match two hours before game time. Any earlier can get you mentally exhausted. Stay away from any physical activity. Try not to watch TV. Stay focused and confident.

One hour before the match, drink a glass of Gatorade. Get to the courts at the bare minimum of forty minutes before playing. Once at the courts, change into your squash clothes. Acknowledge the fact that the change into your squash gear is a mental shift in direction. Start to think you mean business. Remember we constantly need to work on things that get you to the correct state of mind. Always wear a tracksuit while waiting to play.

Make sure you pay attention to details. How tight do you lace your sneakers? Do you prefer a headband or wristband? Do you have a favorite pair of socks? How about a favorite shirt or shorts? If you don't, start finding them. After winning a tough match, save the shirt. This is just an example. Always re-enforce a positive environment. The mental state goes from the inside out.

Thirty minutes before playing is very critical. Start stretching and use visualization to pretend to stretch for shots. After stretching for ten to fifteen minutes, start swinging your racquet and visualize hitting perfect winners. Your mind cannot differentiate visualizing and actually performing a task. So if you visualize yourself making great gets and hitting winners, in your mind you really are. The visualization of playing great can transfer into your squash game.

If there's a court available, hit by yourself. Try to get your length in order. Practice some volleys and drops and angles. Hit at a good pace until you break a slight sweat. Don't overdo it.

At match time take off your tracksuit. During the warm-up watch your opponent hit the ball. See if you can spot any tell-tail signs to anticipate a shot. See how he or she hits a rail and crosscourt. Make sure you hit to good length. Aim for the back corners. Good length can win a match. Step up for some volleys. Try a drop now and then. Practice how to effectively change the pace of the shot. Don't hit the tin! Remember how much preparation you had made starting from the night before and throughout the day to this moment. A great technique is to lead everything to a final moment. This will get you in the habit of focusing all efforts to a starting gun. This transforms into an internal clock where you set the time for liftoff.

Feel your anxiety and know the stored energy you've accumulated is at hand. Realize that your mental state and physical energy is at its height. Memorize this feeling because this is the ZONE the best athletes refer to. Feel the pressure and emotions. This will get that adrenaline flowing. This is good, but try to stay calm so you can think clearly. Win or lose always keep your cool.

Keep practicing match preparation until you master the art of getting yourself to the ZONE. Now it's up to you! Good Luck!

11

The top squash players in the world seem to know where the ball is going before it's actually hit. This is called anticipation. Anticipation can be developed by watching countless shots executed by a variety of players with different styles of play.

A power-hitter will snap his or her wrist differently from a shot-maker. A retriever plays at a slower pace as compared to a constant volleyer. Tall players stretch to shots while short players scramble. By playing different types of players, you will develop a better way of anticipating. Before top professionals ever get ranked on the circuit, you can bet they played every type of player out there. This is what you need to do.

The next step to better anticipating is watching your opponent hit the ball. This means following the ball from your racquet to your opponent's. Never lose track of the ball or where your opponent is. If you ever get the chance to watch the top players in your area play, notice how well they seem to track the ball during the rallies.

The third step is narrowing down possibilities. Realize where you are in comparison to your opponent's position. If you're in the frontcourt, chances are your opponent will drive the ball deep. Knowing this you've eliminated all the frontcourt shots. Trying to anticipate any shot is too much work. Make it easier by narrowing down to what may be the most likely shot your opponent will hit. Narrowing down shots is the best way I know to increase anyone's anticipating ability.

Another critical factor you must keep in mind is how well you're able to keep the ball tight. For example, if your opponent is on the "T" and you hit a weak shot in the middle, guess how many shots he or she can go for? This is a great place to give your opponent control over the whole court and every shot in the book. Remember, the tighter you keep the ball on the walls and in the corners, the easier it is to anticipate your opponent's next shot. Narrow down your opponent's choices by hitting tight shots as well.

One other thing to keep in mind is that you can only anticipate shots you have. If you have a good straight drop, you'll anticipate your opponent's drop. If you have a great crosscourt, you'll anticipate your opponent's crosscourt. This means that you need to develop as many shots in your game as possible.

Lastly, realize response time. If your opponent intercepts your shot in the frontcourt, you have less time to anticipate his or her return. This is obvious. By shortening the contact time and distance it takes for the ball to come off the front wall to his or her racquet, your opponent has, in effect, added pressure by eliminating response time for you to figure out the next shot. This means trouble. This is what great players try to do to one another. So keep the ball deep and try to lengthen the time it takes for your opponent to return your shots. The longer it takes for your opponent to return your shot, the easier it is for you to anticipate where it'll go. The lob is a great way to buy time.

Building great anticipation takes time and experience. Good luck!

#12

The first time I picked up a racquet and started to play I can remember always running after shots. As I got better, I ran less and hit more winners. I realized that every squash player fell into the same pattern.

As a low D player I started out as a retriever. As I learned to control the ball, I started to control the rally. At first it was one rally, then a series of rallies until I could control a game and then the entire match. My improvement reflected where I stood in the D category. I was a retriever at the low end; a mixture of a retriever and shooter in the middle; and primarily a shooter at the top of the class.

This circle repeated itself in the C class and the B class and finally in the A class. With each class the retrieving and shooting had to be a degree better. This is obvious. But, due to lack of experience, I always felt discouraged when I became a renewed retriever entering the next level.

For example, I worked my way up through the C class and became a decent shot-maker. I made my opponents do all the running as I hovered on the T. This was great and who would want to change things. Some players didn't. Others couldn't. I, on the other hand, had a desire to keep getting better. Like most players I didn't stop to think what was really needed to get to the next level. I discovered, the hard way, that it wasn't hitting better shots. That came later. It was making better gets and retrieving the ball throughout the rally until there was time to get back to the T.

Every time I entered a new level, I ran from shot to shot without ever finding time to get back to the T. The first goal for you as you enter a new level is to get to the

T during the rally. Sometimes this is easily said than done. But, this is the first hurdle. After this, keep yourself on the T as long as possible. Once you're able to get back to the T comfortably and continuously, look to hit winners. The resulting conclusion - efficient mobility around the court had to come first.

Learn the best stretching techniques you can. Use weight training for added strength in getting in and out of deep corners faster. Cross training always helps. But, most of all learn how to run efficiently on a squash court. If you run at full speed, you'll never make it to the end of the match. Pace yourself. This is something I also learned the hard way.

The best court mobility training I know is to perform star drills. This is when you position yourself in the middle of the court on the T. You'll notice the six points of the court being the two front corners, the service boxes, and the two back corners. Run from the T to the left front corner. Run in such a way as to count the number of steps it takes you to get to the front corner. You should be able to get there in three to four long steps. Once in front, take a swing as if hitting the ball then back pedal back to the T. Then run to the right front corner; take another swing and back pedal to the T. Twist and run to the left service box and then back to the T. Twist and run to the back left corner and then back to the T. Then go to the right service box and then back to the T. Finally, go to the back right corner and then back to the T. This is one star. Remember that the running style should mimic the way you run in the court during an actual rally. If you're running correctly, you won't be able to hear your steps. So place each step; don't stomp. Concentrate on your braking ability. Do you brake with a single step or several smaller steps? Take my word for it; brake with several small steps. It'll save your knees.

Work your way to four stars. Once you accomplish this, do two sets of four stars. The desired goal is doing four sets of four star drills. As you run the star, imagine hitting the ball as you enter each of the six points. Visualize making great gets at each instance. Designate each of the six points as hot spots. Memorize how well you move to each of the points and then recover to the T. Make your movement graceful. Try to feel the air pass your face as you start breaking into a sweat. Between each set take a minute break and walk around the parameter of the court. Even during this break period notice each of the points as you pass them. When you feel your heart rate begin to slow, dive into the next set.

Squash is a running game. Learn to move around the court smoothly and try to cover as much distance with each step as possible. Have a strong stride and good leg strength. Stretch to stay limber. Keep in mind if you want to get to the next level; be ready to run the ball down. Great gets will give you the confidence you need to hit those great winners. Remember you're playing squash - the ultimate

mind/body sport.

#13

Let's say you're at the peak of your game. You're ready for any challenge match. You think you've covered everything. The match starts and your string breaks. You're forced to use another racquet. Suddenly, your game is off. The shots are not as precise. You go down fighting and knowing you left out one crucial element of your game. You forgot about the importance of having good equipment. The best preparation is only good if you have the best equipment to utilize your maximum potential.

The worst mistake is to sacrifice your game to save a bit of money. I don't recommend buying the best racquet, but I do suggest getting something of high standard. The lowest racquets are practically given away because no one will buy them. Get something a pro is using because the most important piece of equipment is your racquet.

I have found the current selection of racquets overwhelming. Most look and feel the same at the store. I usually ask the salesperson about the best sellers. Whatever racquets they suggest, ask if you can demo the racquets. This means bringing them home for a trial. All good stores have this service. Take advantage of it. Let's say you get three racquets to try. Here's what to check.

Hold the racquet firmly and swing it around as hard as possible. Do this for each of the racquets. Notice the sound of the air as the racquet passes through it. The racquet that makes the least amount of sound will be the most aerodynamic. The most aerodynamic means better engineering quality and less work for a faster swing.

Now examine the weight distribution. Is it head heavy? If it is, it will hit with more power. But, this is not ideal because grip adjustments can offset this. You need to have a well-balanced racquet. A well-balanced racquet gives the player a better feel in the grip. The grip is at the heart of your touch game. Hold the racquet at a 45-degree angle as if hitting a forehand shot. Instead of swinging through like a typical forehand just perform a chopping action. Notice how much the weight of the racquet shifts from the grip to the top of the head and then back down to the grip. In a good racquet you will hardly notice a change.

The next test is to strike the strings of the racquet against the palm of your hand. Move your palm from the bottom of the head to the top. Notice the vibration. The top of the head is where most of the vibration occurs. Especially notice this area when doing this test. The least amount of vibration is better. I have found the new generation of titanium racquets of excellent quality and best ever for vibration control.

Now, look at the frame. The shape of the head is important. The larger the head, the easier it can break. The racquet head should have a good bumper guard. Some chip away with time while others thin like a pencil eraser. The thinning type is better.

The throat of the racquet is important. This is the sensitive area of feedback down the shaft to the grip. This area should be strongest compared to anywhere else in the head. Find the thinnest spot on the rim of the racquet head. If it's in the throat area, it'll break in no time.

The strings and the grip are the direct feedback points of the racquet. Ironically, even the highest quality racquets come with poor grips and strings. Smooth grips are not good. Both should be replaced immediately. When you choose the grip, get one that is has raised ribs and dotted with holes. I have found these grips lasting the longest and having the best feel. Wilson and Pointfore make this type of grip. Furthermore, restring your racquet with the Ashaway XL synthetic 17-gauge gut. It's the best performer I've ever played with.

Once you've tested all the racquets using the above guideline during your demo period, keep in mind that the best racquet is the one that feels most comfortable when hitting the ball. Now let's examine squash shoes.

You should select a squash shoe that feels comfortable. It should have very little heel support and lots of cornering support. It should not elevate you or have a forward lean because of a higher heel as compared to the toes. The ideal squash shoe makes you feel as if running bare-foot. It should have gum rubber for the best court traction. Adidas, Ektelon, Asic Gels and Prince have very good squash shoes. Just a word of advice, don't use your tennis shoes in the squash court. I've seen it many times, and those are the players that twist an ankle. Tennis shoes don't have the cornering support squash demands.

Athletic clothing for squash should be relatively tight, but comfortable to move in. Loose fitting athletic wear will weight you down when wet. Get use to wearing a wristband. Wear a headband and eye guards together. The headband will help prevent the fogging of the eye guards.

In conclusion, select your equipment carefully. Get a titanium racquet that has a great grip and has been restrung with synthetic gut; have good quality squash shoes with low heels and supported for cornering; and wear tight athletic clothing. It's always reassuring to know your equipment is top-notched. Don't get yourself in the position of losing a big match because of a broken string or slippery grip. To win sometimes the slightest edge can matter. Champions know that an edge can be in the equipment. Don't take a chance! The pros don't!

#14

Executing shots and clearing are unique aspects in the game of squash. While many players focus on developing better winners, I suggest a concentrated effort in proper clearing. I state this because I have seen many players hit great shots when not distracted, but whenever a rally gets tight, their shots seem to loose their punch. This is usually caused by a fear of close contact with their opponent. Therefore, proper clearing must take precedence over improving shots.

I have seen many players neglect proper clearing. Some players don't clear at all. Others use more energy getting out of their opponent's way rather than hitting a well-executed shot. Players that over clear have an untapped potential that can be developed.

Since players that over clear are afraid of getting close to their opponents, they tend to hit shots away from themselves. This player hits mostly crosscourt and boasts. Usually, these shots become very accurate over time and should be formidable weapons except that the shot selection has become so predictable their opponent has relative ease in anticipating each shot. This makes it easier for your opponent to beat you. Therefore, over clearing hurts your strategy. Over clearing also depletes stamina a lot faster. This fear must be overcome to become an effective squash player.

Hitting the ball so that contact is avoided with your opponent is easy; but your opponent may not have the fear of close contact. He or she may deliberately welcome a closer exchange of shots. In this scenario the over clearing player is distracted. He or she can't settle into the game. There is a slight hesitation when retrieving shots. Shots are hit into the tin. Lets are called more frequently and your opponent becomes too much to handle. The best remedy for this is to practice the rail drill with a partner.

In this drill you and your partner mimic a rally that is strictly a deep rail hit along the wall. The objective is to get your partner behind you. As the both of you fight for position to stay in front, you'll discover a circular pattern you and your partner will be engaged in. Focusing on this movement during the rail exchange is vital. Try to move quickly and smoothly around each other. Don't be nervous about the occasional brush or bump you'll experience. Get use to it. Sometimes a slight bump or brush gives the both of you a better reference point when striking the ball. Once you start feeling comfortable doing this on one side, change to the other side of the court and repeat the drill. Remember not to hit hard at first.

In no time will the fear of being close to your opponent disappear. Furthermore, your rail and length will get better -- pulling you away from a crosscourt and boasting game. Just be careful not to get so over-confident and get struck by your partner's swing. If this happens, your past fears become justified and return. Start slow and work on intensity only after you start feeling more comfortable.

The excitement of squash is best experienced in close combat. Every player should make an effort to play closer to his or her opponent. If you can hear them breath, you're in a good tactical position. This will undoubtedly lead to better concentration, confidence and balance. My advice is to dive into the thick of things and learn to keep your cool in close quarter battles for the T, you'll be glad you did!

#15

Squash is a game of footwork and racquet control. In simple terms squash is running and striking. If both aspects of the game are perfected, you will achieve the height of your game. In the process of perfecting the two, a player can forget to unite the two and develops a bad habit.

The bad habit of focusing on each separately will make running and hitting uncoordinated. Disjointed running and hitting creates segmented squash. This can carry over into concentration and strategy. To coordinate your running and hitting game you must develop a better way of swinging at the ball on your last step. There is a fine line as far as timing is concerned. You must strike the ball on your last step and then use the momentum of your swing to prepare for the next shot.

For example, in a backhand shot, you should anticipate the shot and get your feet moving first. Wind up keeping the racquet close to your body. This is the inner circle and is ideal for balance. As you approach the strike zone, mentally focus on your steps and try to calculate the distance it will take to get to the ball.

On your final step shift your weight onto your correct right leg then strike the ball before all your body weight has been shifted to that leg. As the ball exits the strike zone off your racquet, continue to watch the ball, but focus on your backhand follow-through. At the end of the follow-through bring the racquet back into the inner circle close to your body. Notice how on all follow-throughs the racquet naturally gravitates to the middle of the court. Don't fight the weight of the racquet. Go with it and begin to shift your weight and turn to the middle of the court with the swing in synchronized motion. This is coordinated running and hitting. The trick is never applying your full body weight at any particular instance during a shot and keeping your racquet close to you in the wind up. Remember not to step through the shot. Your feet on the last step are fixed; it's just the weight distribution that's in continuous motion. You should feel your weight centered only when on the T.

This type of playing will keep your balance and racquet control smooth. Again, smooth running and hitting develops better concentration. Better concentration makes for better strategy. Once you segment your running and hitting, your game and concentration will always lack that something you'll never be able to pinpoint.

My advice is whenever you focus on improving your drop or crosscourt, do it in such a way that you're incorporating motion with the shot. Effective body weight distribution going into and out of the strike zone can only be created while moving. Develop a hitting style that is synchronized with not only the point of impact but also the follow-through. Use momentum to your advantage. Never just stand and hit. If you do, then trying to improve your game will seem elusive.

#16

Shot selection is critical to good squash. Shot selection is not hitting winners; it's making your opponent cover the farthest distances around the court. If we divide the squash court into zones, we can better understand shot selection.

Let's divide the court into frontcourt and backcourt. Keep in mind that the player who stays in front during most of a match is likely to win; and the T is the best place to be between shots. This is a cardinal rule. The next cardinal rule is to keep your opponent in the corners.

The four corners are where a rally will most likely come to its end. The frontcourt comprises two corners, as does the backcourt. You should always aim for the corners when going for a winner. Keeping your opponent in the corners while you're hovering on the T is the best squash scenario. Once you get your opponent into a corner and gain control of the rally, the next best shot is the corner farthest from your opponent. For example, if your opponent were near the front left corner, the best place to send the ball would be the back right corner.

Once you develop the art of maneuvering your opponent, you'll discover that your opponent may retrieve a certain shot in game one but will not be able to get to the same shot in game three. Keeping your opponent on the run will weaken his or her ability to maintain the fight. Your perimeter of possible winners will widen due to this constant attack and weakening of your opponent. Patience is the key.

If you find that you're controlling a rally, realize that there are three ways of keeping your opponent on the run. You can send him or her horizontally across the court from one service box to the next using crosscourt drives; you can send him or her vertically forward and back with straight drops and hard rails or lobs; and you can send him or her diagonally using boasts, drops and crosscourts. In each case your opponent is doing all the running and you have a clear advantage. This doesn't comprise all shot selections, but it does suggest what to keep in mind as a starting reference point for maneuvering an opponent. Look for all possibilities, but try to master these.

In the third instance I describe trapping your opponent in the diagonal corner maneuver, you'll notice that in this situation your opponent will have covered the most distance possible and you will have relative ease hitting to each diagonal corner. Relative ease suggests confidence in executing the correct shot with the highest probability of hitting the kill zone. Therefore set your goal to make your opponent run diagonally as much as possible. Furthermore, diagonal pressure keeps your opponent stretched and off balance while opening the court for you.

Some pros can trap a competitor in this sequence and instead of putting the ball away will hit slightly higher so that the retrieving player will further exhaust more reserves. Younger players with less experience and high energy get trapped in this diagonal sequence becoming frustrated that a less fit player has overcome them. Whenever you find that you're running from shot to shot without gaining control, break off the pursuit immediately.

Between corners and the T is the inevitable rail that needs to be mastered to perfection. The great Geoff Hunt states in his book that when he started playing squash, his father wouldn't allow any shot making other than hitting rails for a period of a year. Geoff Hunt later became eight-time British Open Champion. Take his advice!

Let's examine the role of the tight rail. Good length is the best neutral shot in the game. Players exchange rails until one gets an opportunity to gain control. Good length can help you gain the upper hand, but keeping the ball as close to the wall as possible is by far much more effective. Get your ball tight to the wall rather than deep into the court. Of course, the best rail sticks to the wall as it dies in the back corner. But, this can take too much effort when off balance. A shot hit short but glued to the wall is just as good without the physical exertion of the deep rail. Thus, hitting shorter rails closer to the wall with consistency will develop the openings you need without depleting your stamina in the process.

One final note regarding shot selection is exploiting a poorly executed shot by your opponent. For example, if your opponent hits a bad shot in the middle of the court, is it wise to select a shot that will give your opponent a clear path for retrieval? The answer is no! You should hit the shot that put you directly in your opponent's way. The reasoning is that if your opponent sets you up for a winner, you are entitled to go for the best possible winner and your opponent must be penalized by retrieving the next shot even if it means running around you. If you find yourself in this situation and your opponent runs directly at you and asks for a let, state that he or she set you up for a winner. Add that it's their responsibility to make every effort to get the next shot even if this means running around you. In short, whenever you have the advantage, hit shots that make your opponent run around you as a penalty.

Use shot selection to weaken your opponent. Weaken your opponent by making him or her do all the running while you control the T. Make your opponent run diagonally as much as possible. Use the hidden rule of squash to penalize your opponent by making him or her run around you when you have the advantage. Remember to try to hit shorter rails that stick to the wall rather than deep length to help save your stamina. Both shot-makers and retrievers can gain a valuable insight if they focus on proper shot selection as part of their game.

#17

As a youth I discovered that top squash professionals rallied unlike the typical club player. They were steady at one point and attacked at another. I noticed a pattern I call "attacking and regrouping". Once I tried this tactic on some of my opponents, I found my game less predictable. I also noticed my opponents waiting for my next wave of attacking shots.

This meant I began to control the tempo of the match. This also meant that my opponents were making a critical error –

they were playing my game. When I had them in the grips of playing my game, I discovered that I didn't need to hit winners. I could control the match by setting the tempo. This led to mentally breaking down my opponents.

Sometimes this sort of "attacking and regrouping" worked, other times I got too tired or frustrated that I couldn't end the rally. With experience I realized that I didn't need to win the rally in the attacking phase. I realized I needed to attack a certain number of shots and then needed to fall back into a length game. I also realized that picking a certain number of shots kept me from exhausting my stamina. If you don't pace yourself correctly, this strategy will never become effective.

Remember when I refer to attacking, I suggest a quicker exchange of shots making your opponent stretch a little harder for each get. Just add pressure with tempo rather than great shooting. Making your opponent rush and unable to think about the next shot is attacking with tempo.

Again, you must develop an attacking game for no more than three to four shots and then try to regroup by hitting tight rails. Incorporating a three or four shot attacking assault and learning to pull out of this self-imposed barrage into a slower and steadier style takes practice. This can only be done when a player is in control and finds an opportunity to implement such a strategy. Finding the right opportunity comes with the experience of trial and error. It all starts when you attack your opponent's initial weak return.

It is certain that the "attack and regrouping" tactics can be part of your game no matter what your level. The medium between attacks is hitting good length, which should be perfected first. But, you should avoid excessive length.

Excessive length shots are those steady rails and/or crosscourts to good length for a succession without changing your pace. It can feel like being in cruise control. This can be a good strategy to a point. The danger lies in playing this safe game to the extreme. Length should only be maintained until your opponent hits a weak return. This is the ideal moment to apply pressure not to end the rally, but to suck your opponent into your attacking game. But, keeping your opponent guessing is crucial. Keep in mind that you want to make your opponent realize that whenever he or she hits a loose shot, you will attack with intensity and not really go for a winner. There is a unique difference.

Hitting a great shot puts pressure on you even if you have a great set-up. Picking up the tempo adds pressure only to your opponent both physically and mentally. You must adjust your focus not on a single shot but the tempo to add pressure. One outlook is concentrated on a single event while the other seems to change the climate.

The mental pressure of applying such a game plan will weaken your opponent's resolve to challenge your attacks. When you break down your opponent's defenses to the point of conceding the match, the match will be in your control and declared mentally over for your opponent.

#18

The most important element of your squash game is your stroke. There are several areas we need to discuss regarding a proper squash stroke.

First, you need to find your particular sweet spot. This has nothing to do with the racquet. It is the specific area of contact in the motion of the swing that produces your maximum punch. Depending on your height, weight and athleticism, this point can vary. No one has the same favorite point of contact. Discovering this point will be the best thing you'll ever do for your overall squash game. But, keep in mind that it may take years to fine-tune your swing so that this point actually reveals itself. The best method in discovering your particular sweet spot is practicing alone.

Second, once you discover your sweet spot, you must shorten your swing. The shortest swing that can get the same job done will undoubtedly use less time and energy for shot execution. Furthermore, this means you'll have a better attacking game when you need it. So compact your stroke by remembering to keep your elbow in and to use your wrist as much as possible. Raise your shoulders, making your head position lower between them. Keep your knees bent and stay in the crouch position. A good practice technique is to crouch and have your elbow and knee meet at the point of contact with the ball. Not all players can do this. But, with time and with good footwork, it can be done. Practicing volleys can also help shorten your swing. But, the wrist is the best mechanism in getting your swing and power to potential.

The third element of the squash stroke is your grip. Your hand can squeeze tightly and loosen on command. In squash, the control you have over your grip is crucial when making contact with the ball. A tight grip at the exact point of contact and then a looser grip in the follow-through are the desired goal. You must be aware of your sense of touch to attain this kind of grip coordination. Your racquet control will be at its best if you can sense when to tighten and loosen your grip during a stroke. Some players like a relatively tight grip throughout the stroke. Most pros will recommend this in the front of the court when time is restricted and when optimum control is needed or in a full power shot. But overall, a constant tight grip will weaken your arm as the match progresses. Learning to tighten your grip at the point of impact takes practice and conscious effort.

The secret in practicing alone is to isolate a specific aspect of your swing. A player can practice grip control in one session, and in another try to focus on a more compact swing.

Finally, keep in mind that all squash players have two types of strokes that need an equal amount of attention. You must incorporate and develop all three elements of the squash swing to both your backhand and forehand!

The sweet spots, compactness and grip may vary considerably for both the backhand and forehand. Therefore, developing each side evenly over the course of your squash progression will undoubtedly be a challenge. Your test is to keep both sides balanced as you chart your course through the higher levels of play. Not an easy test! So keep in mind, a great forehand means more backhand practice to balance the sides and visa versa. Both sides must be equal in strength and shot control not only today but also a year from now. My advice is to keep everything evenly balanced at all times by practicing each of the six areas - one at a time.

If an uneven backhand or forehand develops, as it most likely will, your overall squash strategy will be affected. For example, a strong forehand and weak backhand will affect the way you concentrate. Keep in mind a weaker backhand will subconsciously make you look more attentively for backhand protection. Once this happens, you're immediately in the defensive by defending your backhand more so than your forehand.

When both strokes are equal in strength, only then can you focus on building an effective squash strategy. The pros know this is the only way to play squash at its best!

#19

All of us know that squash is a unique sport. And this uniqueness can warrant a different level of interest for each squash player attracted to the sport. Usually, the more a player plays squash, the more he or she likes it.

Nevertheless, all squash players vary in the way they pursue their squash activities. Some play once a week, while others can't help to get on the court everyday. A select few will play twice a day. This interest can evolve into something more. Squash can evolve into an obsession. And I've discovered age makes no difference when it comes to the birth of a squash addict.

If you're the player that's driven to play as much squash as possible, and it may seem at times that everyone just plays squash while you're engrossed in it. Don't worry. I know how you feel. What you're doing is great! I can think of worst things to do.

Keep in mind that you're the player that energizes all squash activities. Wherever you are in the world, you're a welcomed inspiration to the sport. The pros know this and love to hear you're just as addicted to squash as they are. It will ignite both your fires for the game when you tell them. So tell them whenever you get the chance.

I can also assure you that you're not alone. There is a select group of players covering all the far corners of the squash world. This message is for you - the squash fanatic who loves this game, and has made it a permanent part of his or her schedule.

Here are fifteen rituals for my fellow squash fanatic to follow.

1.   Start running more. If you can find a hill, run up and jog down. This is the best type of running for squash because it keeps you in the tuck position, and mimics stop and go action. This is great for leg endurance and power.

2.   Bike more. Ride a bike for 20 miles twice a week to build up the legs. If you don't like to bike then do the row machine. It's the best machine for squash. This will get your legs stronger while saving your joints.

3.   **Start swimming twice a week. Swim in the morning. This means spending an hour in the pool doing as many laps as possible. Distances should be according to your ability. This will build breathing control and develop better lung capacity as well as save your joints from overuse.**

4.   **Get as many professional squash videos as you can and watch a championship match on video two times a week. Watching the best will only motivate you to improve.**

5.   **Plan on playing at least six tournaments over the course of the year. Playing in tournaments will help you in**

match preparation and get you mentally tough.

6.   Camps are beneficial during the off-season only if a good crop of players attends your session.

7.   Make sure to read about proper nutrition so that you're eating correctly. Only the right fuel will give you the red line performance you'll need.

8.   Read some books on squash and sports psychology. Remember squash is the ultimate mind/body game. Keep your mind as well as your body up to date with the latest and the best techniques.

9.   Play in your local squash league. This will involve challenge matches from

teammates to defend your position as well as playing against other club players. This is the best way to gauge your level of play and to set goals.

10.   Make sure you get enough rest to avoid injuries. This means playing and training hard for three weeks and almost nothing but practicing alone and stretching after each session on the fourth week. If you don't listen to your body especially when it needs rest, squash will be a one-way ticket to one of your worst injuries.

11.   Play at least four matches per week and practice for a minimum of thirty minutes three times during your hard

weeks. Try practicing alone in the morning and play in the evening. Practicing alone works great before a swim or long bike ride. If you don't practice, you'll never develop great shots.

12.   Do star drills illustrated in the KhanSquash tips every time you're at the courts, especially after matches. As you run through the drill visualize hitting the ball at each point of the star. Four sets of four stars should work. Star drills will mimic the movements in a match. Therefore, it's the best training you could possibly do.

13.   Find a good coach and take some lessons. A good coach has won

tournaments in the past; has taught squash for at least five years; and has an eye for seeing your talents.

14.   Pay especial attention to your equipment. Choose your racquet and sneakers carefully. These are the two most important things for squash.

15.   Learn to focus your mind by meditating or doing yoga. The best mediation for squash is hitting alone without distraction and using plenty of visualization.

Remember everyone else says it's just a game! But we know better!

See you on the court!

20

We are repeatedly told to watch the ball to the point of contact and to watch our opponents as he or she hits the ball. This method of watching is told to further improve our anticipation. Better anticipation is said to gives us a jump on the next shot. All is true. But, there are times when you can't see the ball or your opponent. These are called the "blind spots".

Here's a typical squash scenario.

An opponent serves deep into a backhand corner. A blind spot will occur when the receiver twists to hit a standard rail length return. There are two things to keep in mind during this episode. The first is how the receiver will interpret the last peripheral sight of the server before executing the shot, and the second is what the opponent will do during the blind spot.

First, as the receiver focuses on the ball to hit the backhand rail, the server has the advantage because he or she can move undetected. As receiver focuses on the ball and watches it drop into the corner, his peripheral vision will see the server in the corner of his eye. If I were the server, I would move toward the receiver's backhand side as he began to twist into the backhand corner. Once I realize the receiver has stepped into the shot and the blind spot is initiated, I will silently move back to the forehand side. Why?

From the receiver's perspective the last image of me is moving over to the backhand to cover the rail length return. Realizing that I'll be on top of the next shot, the receiver will try to outsmart me by hitting a different shot. Let's say he hits a boast believing that if I'm hovering for a backhand return that the boast off the sidewall will land furthest from me in the front forehand court.

However, during the blind spot I've moved to the forehand side of the court. The boast return will feed into my racquet for a drop winner. I've exploited the blind spot to my advantage. This may not happen all the time, but the point is to attempt to do something unexpected during a blind spot situation. Timing is critical. If done correctly, this will put added pressure on your opponent.

Using the same squash scenario, let's say instead of having my opponent peripherally observe me moving over to the backhand, I deliberately stay in the service box area. My opponent, using his last images of me as a reference point, will undoubtedly try to hit a rail so that not to feed me. I, on the other hand, will wait until he starts his shot execution. Once out of sight, I will speed over to the backhand side of the court for quick cut off.

Here I have changed my opponent's game plan by exploiting his peripheral vision and blind spot to my advantage.

Another example is when a player hits a great boast to fully stretch his or her opponent. As the opponent moves up to get the boast, the other player can move up behind his or her opponent until the blind spot occurs. The opponent's last peripheral sight was that the other player was coming up from behind for a drop. The opponent is forced to lob or crosscourt since a drop is what is expected. If the other player has exploited the blind spot correctly, he or she will not be on their opponent's heels but will fade back at the last second to hit a quick volley as his or her opponent feeds the ball. The opponent is taken completely by surprise.

Using this scenario again, Let's make the player not appear to follow his or her opponent up. Let's deliberately stay back and have the last peripheral view showing the player on the T. As the opponent focuses in on the boast retrieval, the blind spot is initiated and the last image of the other player was back on the T. The opponent will drop the ball thinking the other player is too far back to make a good get. The other player, meanwhile, will stay on the T until his or her opponent is in the midst of the blind spot to start silently forward. When the opponent hits the drop, the other player will pounce on it driving it deep to the back of the court. Again, the opponent is taken completely by surprise.

Peripheral vision will undoubtedly eliminate most blind spots. Nevertheless, the fact remains that whenever your opponent is turned away from you in the corners, during crosscourts, and when they're in front that blind spots occur. As you become a better observer of what your opponent sees, you will discover the realistic use of blind spot attacks.

The top pros use blind spots as the best time to catch his or her opponent off guard. Usually, when you begin to exploit this type of strategy, you'll find your opponent less at ease when you're not in his or her peripheral sight. His or her concentration becomes unstable and you start to control the rally. Once you gain momentum, you become less concerned with hitting great shots, but rather start to hit more shots that get you out of your opponent's peripheral view.

As you move up in rank, you'll need to create blind spots. Once you realize that a blind spot episode is about to occur, you must plan your movements accordingly to fully exploit and fool your opponent during such events. On the other hand, when you become victim to a blind spot, use every sense of awareness to track your opponent's movements.

During blind spots I have been astonished to discover opponents silently crouched next to me or even three feet from the front wall volleying my shot into the nick. Pros wait for such blind spots to initiate an attack. It can prove to be mentally devastating.

When you become invisible for that split second during the blind spot, you become a formidable attacker at any level of squash. Start to use blind spots as a weapon in your game because I can guarantee they'll be used against you.

21

There are two types of squash strategies. One is the offensive attacking game, and the other is the patient defensive game. The offensive game is primarily all imaginable squash shots close to the floor of the court. The defensive game is primarily all imaginable squash shots that linger up high in the court. One strategy uses the lower court area while the other focuses on the upper court area. The lower court encompasses 75% of all squash shots, while the upper court utilizes only 25% of all squash shots. To build a strong overall squash game, we need to focus on the often-neglected upper court.

Two things need to be kept in mind when concerning the upper court. The first is learning to utilize the upper area by hitting shots that have high contact points on the front wall. The second is returning a shot that lingers in the upper area of the court. One is execution - the other is retrieving.

The best upper court shot is the lob. Therefore, the lob must be perfected! This shot is best executed from the front of the court. Usually when retrieving a high drop or boast.

When hitting a lob, make sure it makes contact with the front wall approximately one meter above the service line. Also, try to hit crosscourt lobs at first. A good lob has a significant arc. Since the purpose of upper court shots is to extend the time between exchanges, the ball should linger in the air as long as possible. The lobbed ball should deflect off the sidewall one meter from the back wall.

Because the lob can die in the back corner, the lob can become one of the most devastating shot in your arsenal. If executed correctly, the lob will get you back to the T. The lob can also break you out of any fast paced rally by abruptly changing the tempo.

The difficulty regarding the lob is that it can't be practiced alone. Of course, one can try, but it should be combined in a sequence of shots using a rail, a boast and then a lob. It's important to keep the ball warm or else your touch will be off. But, practicing with two players is easy. One player boasts while the other lobs. The ball remains warm, and the rapid succession of attempts only improves your accuracy.

The next shot is the crosscourt that deflects high off the sidewall into your opponent. This shot should only be attempted when your opponent is in the backcourt and close to the sidewall. If this type of crosscourt is hit when your opponent is in front, he or she can volley it before the ball reaches the deflection point. Also, if your opponent is not next to the sidewall and more in the middle, he or she can let the ball go to the back wall. If this happens, you become trapped as the path of the ball revolves into the middle of the backcourt.

These are just two examples of the types of shots you can use in the upper area of the court. In short, any high shot that lingers out of your opponent's reach, namely his or her sweet spot, will have the same effect.

The main points are that upper court shots change the pace, get you back in position, and use less energy. In the long run, you'll confuse your opponent, add pressure by getting back to the T more efficiently, and have more stamina for the rest of the match. Although this sounds easy, upper court shots require a great deal of accuracy and timing. Practicing is the first step. The next is to make a conscious effort to use upper court shots during a match.

Remember to stay cool and maintain good concentration at all times. Championship squash starts in your head. Only then can you effectively incorporate tactics.

When attempting upper court shots, notice the lag time between exchanges. Observe how the rhythm is interrupted. Also, become aware of your opponent's reaction. Discover how the soft arc of a lob can add tremendous pressure during a point.

Let's change scenarios. If your opponent attempts to use this strategy against you, remember that upper court shots are your opponent's way of getting back in position. You need to keep yourself out of the danger by reciprocating with an upper court shot yourself. As your opponent tries to buy time and gets you out of position, you need to buy time with a lingering upper court shot to neutralize his or her attempt for control of the rally.

Although, lower court shots like a drop and a boast can slow the pace, upper court shots like the lob and high crosscourts are better ways of getting back to the T after a blistering exchange of fast shots.

Winning a point using devastating power and fast exchanges can feel great. But, keep in mind that the best players can not only hit with sustained fast pace but also can lob and use the upper court to retain position. Besides, Pace falls drastically behind Position by comparison in a squash professional's rulebook. Furthermore, winning a single rally is not the goal – it's winning the match!

So, don't sacrifice 25% of your squash game by neglecting the upper court area. Believe me, it will eventually come back to haunt you. My advice is to build a stronger squash game by using high upper court shots as part of your strategy starting today.

22

There is a single shot in squash that stops your opponent in his tracks. It creates astonishment even from otherwise unbiased referees. It can make a silent gallery of spectators leap with applause. It can boost your energy and dissipate your opponent's. It is the shot to strive for as far as winners are concerned. I'm talking about the spectacular nick.

A nick can be described as a shot that deflects off the front wall where the ball's trajectory is so severely angled that the ball strikes close to where the sidewall and floor meet. Keep in mind that if the objective is to get the ball as close as possible to where the sidewall and floor meet that the angle must be calculated not only how far horizontally the ball must travel but also vertically. The combination of the two should create a downward angle. There is a hint of a slice in the shot to help steer the ball into this downward angle.

The nick by definition is the meeting point of the standing walls and the floor throughout the perimeter of the court. This fact attests to the wide variation in the types of nicks a player can attempt.

This is also the reason why the nick is one of the most creative shots in squash. It can appear as a delicate drop nick or as a crushing slice volley into the nick. If executed correctly, a nick is the finest way to end a long rally.

Hitting the nick on command borders a higher plateau in the touch game. A player capable of regularly hitting the nick denotes the precision of a craftsman.

Like all craftsmen the tools, the materials and the environment are in direct relation to the end product. This is no less the case for nicks. With ample practice, a good racquet, and a nice court with uniform walls much like the new ASB courts, the potential for the nick is greater. Yet, the most crucial factor is the set-up. A squash player capable of hitting nicks must have that certain set-up for successful completion of the shot. Spotting a potential nick is half the battle. Once that's done, actually hitting the nick is next.

In some nicks the ball has a trickling bounce with some sort of hope for the other guy. Other nicks are hit so well that there's not even a hint of a bounce and the ball literally rolls off the sidewall. These are rare.

Again, hitting a nick is all about the angle or trajectory of the ball off the front wall – not your racquet. The easiest nicks are located in the two front corners. Designate these areas as your initial target zones.

Unlike all other shots, the nick comes from the heart. You must feel the nick a split second before hitting it. Visualizing perfect nicks can help a great deal. Let's take it a step further. Create a vivid scenario in your mind.

Envision yourself as a hunter stalking the court for the chance to kill a nick. You must look for it at all times. It must become an obsession.

You must experiment by hitting nicks from all angles of the court and find your personal target zones. Start with the two front corners but then expand to the rest of the court. Remember the nick first begins by spotting an opportunity. The best opportunities are when you force your opponent to hit the ball in the middle of the court. Keep in mind that the angle into the nick is the key. Internal alarms should alert you when nick opportunities reveal themselves. Be on the lookout and be ready to fire! In short, you must chisel the nick concept into your mind and keep it with you during every rally of a match.

Executing a nick is regarded as either courageous or foolish. This depends on whether the nick attempt is hit well or not. If hit well - you feel like a champion. When it misses, your opponent is usually set-up for a winner. This is the foremost reason why players avoid trying the nick shot. The fear of setting up your adversary and looking like the fool who took the gamble can eliminate any kind of nick attempt from your mind.

My advice is to get rid the fear and keep trying! But, it's a fact that when you miss a nick attempt, you'll pay. This fact should not instill fear, but should make your attempt that much better. However, one thing does happen after your first nick attempt - your opponent realizes he or she is playing a unique kind of shooter. With this realization he or she will make every effort to prevent your next attempt.

Every pro knows that a successful nick can be a displacing moment for your opponent. It is characterized as a temporary elevation for the player who hits the nick. This elevation, although temporary, can breakdown the mentally toughest competitors.

The pros hold the nick shot in esteem. Although, all pros practice the nick shot, some hit it well while others seem to struggle. In the Khyber Pass area, which is my family's place of origin, the high altitude keeps the ball in play forever. The squash players there discovered early that the nick was the fastest way to kill the ball, especially against some of the fittest players in the world.

Although it's the best shot in the sport, no one has found an effective way of teaching it. This is primarily due to the lack of importance given to the shot, and the desire lacked by most squash players to add it into his or her repertoire. It can be one of the hardest shots to learn, but it's not out of reach. The secret is to make it one of your personal missions in squash.

Once the nick becomes part of your game, it will make all your other shots seem ordinary. You will have scratched the realm of the squash wizards like Qamar Zaman, one of the finest nick masters ever. Yet, Zaman and other nick masters will admit that the nick, while being the deadliest weapon in their arsenal, can betray you. Nevertheless, the nick became one of their legendary strokes. Make it one of yours.

As we speak, the squash courts in the Khyber Pass are being riddled with nicks by some of the best up-and-coming professionals in the sport. What's good for them is good for you! Make it a habit of going for the nick! Or else all your shots will just be ordinary!

#23

If you've decided to get serious about squash then you'd better understand the T. The T is located in the middle of the court where the serve boxes meet. The T is characterized as the best offensive and the best defensive position between shots. With all this said, there's one aspect of being on the T that's often over-looked. The key is how to use the T to set-up traps and create a tactical advantage. But before we start addressing the T, we need to understand a bit more about squash.

Squash is a game of tactics. These tactics incorporate hitting the ball, moving correctly and watching. In squash terminology, it's your stroke execution, footwork and anticipation. All of these areas need a staging point. The best staging point is the T. Once a player realizes the importance of this fact and the T's relevance in squash, something seems to happen at the higher levels where the rallies are longer and more intense.

At the higher levels of squash it's easier to get a feel for your opponent. What I mean is that, you start to observe patterns in your opponent's game and you inadvertently learn to decipher his or her weaknesses. You start thinking like your opponent. You even feel like you can get inside your opponent's head and start to sense what he or she will do next. In this realm the match is won not on the court but in the minds of the players. In essence, you get to know the person you're playing and can decode his or her game. This bonding isolates the players where the universe is limited to the court and the ensuing battle is the all-important event at hand.

At the higher levels squash players use their instincts. Once this happens, players discover how to read their opponent's instincts and only then will a player's game transform from technique and fitness to the mental sphere. Once there, a player realizes that only with instincts and wits is he or she capable of outsmarting his or her opponent. One way to use your instincts is by setting traps. The best place to set traps is from the T. Only with this understanding of the mental game in squash can the T be fully exploited for a winning strategy. And this is when squash gets really interesting.

But because squash is a game of technique, one cannot overlook the fact that squash requires hours of practice and training so that a player's instincts can be activated and fully mature. I encourage every player to get to this place. It's not easy, but with the right training and focus, it's within sight. Now let's talk about how the T is used by the pros.

Let's say you're in a tight match with a player of equal level. The rallies are long and intense. The player who better uses the T to his or her advantage will win the match. That's right. I said, "Uses the T", not "recovers to the T" faster or more efficiently.

If an experienced player sees his or her opponent not recovering to the T correctly, it calls for an offensive shot. Usually at the start of a match both players are fresh and recovery to the T is unwavering. But, once either player shows the first signs of fatigue, then recovery to the T is less efficient and room for error occurs. Therefore the best exploitation of the T can only be accomplished once a softening up period has elapsed. This is when the pros use the

T to influence his or her tiring opponent's shots.

How can one use the T to manipulate his or her opponent's shots? The simple rule regarding the T is that, any player who stands directly on top of the T before his or her opponent hits the ball is likely to get a defensive shot from his or her opponent. This is the key. What if you stand more a bit to the right of the T? Your opponent is likely to try to pass you down the line on your backhand (for a right-handed player). If you stand a bit to the left, your opponent is likely to go down the line to your forehand or

crosscourt, driving you to a back corner.
These are typical scenarios. Now let's do
these types of maneuvers on purpose
making your opponent think you've
recovered to the T late and out of position.
This type of hoax is used by the pros at
times to make his or her opponent believe
he or she is set up to hit a good shot when
in actuality the opponent is being set up
for a trap.

I know it sounds a bit sneaky, but all of us
know winning and losing in squash is
personal and when you can set up a trap,
you'll do anything to see it through. After
all, this kind of thinking is an important

part of building your mental game and should be used to weaken your opponent's mental game.

Think about it. Once you've executed a successful hoax from the T and your opponent realizes he or she has fallen into a trap, your opponent will begin to doubt the way he or she is anticipating your actions. Once that enters the mind of any squash player, especially in a tense battle, then focusing on game strategy takes a turn for the worse. This could be the edge needed to win an otherwise equally contested match.

Another example is making your opponent feel you've committed to his or her shot in a certain way. This is different from standing incorrectly on the T to force a certain shot. Committing means moving to a shot in advance. Usually this type of hoax works best when your opponent is behind you in a corner while you're on the T. As your opponent winds up to hit a shot, make he or she think you see a rail shot coming and drop back a bit as if to retrieve the shot off the back wall. Your opponent should have ample warning of your commitment. He or she will respond by hitting something like a boast to the frontcourt. As your opponent steps into the shot, use the blind spot opportunity to change directions and shift forward. Keep in mind this works best after you've become familiar with your opponent's game and he or she is beginning to tire. If things go as planned, you should be at the front court hitting a drop winner while your opponent thinks you've committed and moved back for a drive.

An additional example is when your opponent is in the backhand corner and you initiate a move to the right creating the impression that you think your opponent is going crosscourt with the ball. Your opponent will respond not by going for the typical rail to wrong foot you, but he or she will try to hit the shot harder to pass you. You will have given your opponent the false impression of committing to his or her shot incorrectly. With the ball now traveling back to you at a faster pace, you will have created an opening by moving correctly to intercept the rail and cut off the ball sooner than expected, trapping your opponent behind you. Your commitment hoax in this case caused a tempo change in your favor.

Keep in mind that manipulating your opponent like this takes practice and split second timing, which means it can back fire if done incorrectly. The bottom line is to make sure you're good enough before ever making an attempt. You'll know when it's time.

Winning in squash will need a variety of tactics depending on the type of player you are and the types of players you come across. But, one thing is certain - your opponent will hit shots that you're least prepared to return. Learn not only to disguise your shots but also learn to disguise your movements. The way you commit to a shot and the way you position yourself on the T can both be manipulated to lure an unsuspecting opponent into a trap.

Knowing this early in your squash development could be critical. The pros use these types of hoaxes because it's one of the best ways to win the mental battle. So start using the T not just as the best point of recovery, but also as the most likely place to manipulate your opponent's next shot.

#24

In squash playing offensively means taking the initiative to win a rally by applying more pressure. Applying more pressure means making it more difficult for your opponent to return shots. The determining factor in the way you can apply pressure will depend on your level and your opponent's capability to defend. These factors can vary, but the ways you can apply pressure don't.

There are three ways to apply pressure in squash. The first is making an opponent retrieve a difficult shot. The second is shortening the actual time between exchanges forcing an opponent to rush. The third is combining both tactics by making an opponent retrieve a difficult shot with the least amount of time to prepare.

The first method can be described as a shot-maker's strategy. A shot-maker goes for winners given any opportunity. This type of strategy keeps an opponent under constant pressure. In essence, the shot-maker makes his or her opponent do most of the running. Yet, this type of pressure is ineffective against an agile and fitter opponent.

The second method of adding pressure is attacking the ball not so much to hit the winner but to return the ball in the shortest amount of time. Here the attacker uses the half volley (striking the ball close to the floor after its first bounce) and volley (striking the ball in the air before hitting the floor) to intercept his or her opponent's shots as quickly as possible. The aim is to keep the other player under constant pressure by eliminating time to think about the next shot.

A player who likes being in front can easily incorporate this strategy. By intercepting shots off the front wall as quickly as possible, a player can maintain pressure by stepping up the pace and eliminating the lag time between exchanges. This type of player is determined to keep you off balance as he or she dominates the T.

The best counter in both of these strategies is slowing the pace down with lobs, high rails and high crosscourts into the back corners. Slowing the pace will make it easier to get back in position and will lengthen the time between exchanges.

This can destroy an attacker's game plan. Although, attempting this maneuver against a player who likes to volley and stay in front can be difficult. Furthermore, a player who prefers the second type of adding pressure is usually in good shape and can go the distance. Nevertheless, the Achilles heel in this type of player is that he or she lacks patience at a slower pace.

The third type of pressure assimilates both methods described above. Here the player will recover to the T in the least amount of time; will try to hit winners given the slightest opening; and will intercept every shot as quickly as possible. This is easily said than done. But it is possible to attain this level of play. Unfortunately, you may have run into this type of player. He or she is usually the first seed in tournaments.

Perfecting offensive strategy is one of the most important goals for all squash professionals. Professionals realize that positioning, shot-making and fast exchanges need to be synchronized so that optimal performance can be achieved. Therefore, make it a priority in your game.

Regardless of level, a player must take the initiative to add pressure and win critical points during a match. Since everyone has a unique style in squash, learning to apply pressure is as unique as the way you play. Eventually, you will grasp this concept. Once this happens, you will have discovered the key element in creating your best wins. Keep in mind it only takes a few good wins to get seeded in the next tournament. My advice is to make those wins and get seeded. Then you'll feel pressure without being on the court. If you discover how to control this type of pressure, please let me know. But don't worry. This type of pressure is worth it. It comes with being the first seed.

#25

At the core of a squash player's best performance there is a single flaw. It will remain hidden until the most unlikely time. It can occur at the beginning as well as at the end of matches. It can ruin a winning sequence of shots. It can give any opponent the confidence to challenge. It is considered the first sign of mental breakdown. It is the one thing that you should avoid at all costs. What I am referring to is called the unforced error.

The unforced error is defeat defined in a single episode. The unforced error is the single flaw that eliminates the chance of becoming a champion. It is not the error that determines this fact. It is the type of error that has occurred.

An unforced error is the inability to execute. The inability to complete an action must be accompanied by some sort of resistance to validate it on the squash court. If there is no resistance or pressure to force you into the error, then you're not mentally tough enough to attain the top levels of squash. Hitting an unforced error is allowing your mind to lapse. This is why it is a sign of mental weakness. No one is immune to unforced errors. What is important is to keep the frequency at your absolute minimum.

There is one aspect of the unforced error that is shared in common with all players. And that is no coach can help you get rid of it. No matter what your level, all players must realize that avoiding the unforced error must be remedied in a uniquely personal way. Finding your remedy could be all that you need to get on the path of becoming a championship player.

Some have suggested that the unforced error is associated with fear or nervousness. Others have mentioned that it is caused by lack of attention or no desire to win. Still more state that it can be linked with fatigue. All are legitimate causes. Nevertheless, the unforced error must have your full attention, in that you must vanquish it from your mind and game. If it occurs, never dwell on it. Accept it as part of a test to keep you on track. Just remember if it occurs too often, you'll boost your opponent's confidence and diminish your own. It is the single event that can initiate a downward spiral ending up as one of your worst defeats. All of us know that the worst of defeats is when a player is distracted and can't get his or her head into a match. The biggest distraction of all is the unforced error.

The best remedy for the unforced error is taking the time to practice alone. Making this critical step will be one of the best things you can do to improve faster and build that needed confidence in shot execution. With this new and improved confidence you'll have fewer unforced errors and more winning shots.

One of the worst feelings on the court is hearing the sigh of a packed gallery of spectators as they witness one of your unforced errors in the heat of a great point. Don't wait for that moment to decide to eliminate unforced errors from your game.

#26

I've seen many professional players hit the squash ball harder than ever believed possible. I've witnessed and endured a string of hard shots that astonished me. Although power is critical to championship squash, it is not the deciding factor, especially in the front court. The front court is the claimed territory of the touch player. This player masters the most difficult and most elegant of all shots. The touch player is known to crush an opponent's spirit with a single shot. His or her deadliest weapon is called the drop. And the secret is in the technique.

Accuracy is needed to hit the most delicate of shots on the squash court. The most delicate of all shots is the drop, and it demands pinpoint accuracy to be effective. Every player knows that a bad attempt at the drop is an instant opening for an opponent. This is why a touch player tries to extend fully, and holds the racquet almost parallel to the floor, to create that needed pinpoint accuracy. The only way to perform this kind of extension and racquet control is to have great anticipation and flexibility. Moreover, the touch player likes getting as close as possible to the front wall. The closer he or she can get to the target area, the more precise the shot. This is a great rule of thumb for anyone trying to improve his or her drop. But, this is just one part of the puzzle. Correct movement is also important.

To perform the touch drop a player needs to get very low by keeping the legs apart. Running to the ball is transformed into a series of long stretches, ending in a near split at the point of intercepting the ball for the drop. He or she stretches to the fullest in the exact moment the ball is about to hit the floor. As he or she stretches to the front court, the ball is then lifted, ever so slightly, to just above the tin. The ball then brushes the front wall so delicately that it barely seems to make it over the lip extension of the tin.

The touch player is a master of moving with blinding speed and then suddenly stopping. When the forward momentum and stopping action perfectly counteract one another, the result is an intensely focused point of balance. This creates the stillness and accuracy needed to execute the best drops. The bad thing about this maneuver is that a player instinctively holds his or her breath at the focused point of balance.

This instinctive breathing control is automatically activated whenever we demand accuracy. Think of it as a sniper before he pulls the trigger. Steadiness for accuracy becomes directly related to how still and focused the shooter can be. Sometimes the best way for the mind and body to get still and gain better focus is to stop breathing. It is usually the final procedure before initiating a kill.

This type of breathing control also attributes to the fact that the great touch players throughout history have not been the fittest. They rely mostly on the front court touch shots, which need many focused points of balance that restrict their breathing.

The body and mind have a unique relationship in squash. There is a continuous struggle in the body to oxygenate the blood with the help of the lungs. If the breathing is smooth, the oxygen intake is uniform. Once a player interrupts his or her breathing pattern, two things seem to happen.

The first is that the lungs work harder. The lungs strain to compensate for the sudden loss. It may take several hard breaths to get your lungs back on track.

As your lungs make the necessary adjustment, you mind gets distracted. As this innate survival instinct kicks in, strategy to win deviates.

The second is that the player may also need to slow down. The combination of breathing harder and slowing down can get a player back in the point in the least amount of time. However, when a pro senses this happening to his or her opponent, it is a signal to attack. This is why smooth breathing is essential for concentration on the squash court and to keep an opponent from attacking. This testifies to the fact that professionals try to move, breath and concentrate as smoothly as possible throughout the duration of a tough match.

But, all of us get tired at some point of the match. Professionals know this so they also try to master the art of camouflaging fatigue. Professionals will try to appear relaxed and calm as long as possible. If a bout of hard breathing is necessary, he or she will take deeper breaths when turned away from his or her opponent. Although, this doesn't seem to work in the new all glass courts where reflections hide nothing.

It's obvious that the best kill shot in the frontcourt is the drop. When a touch player develops his or her deadly drop, it can be one of the most gracefully executed shots seen on the court. It's as if the rest of the game must yield to the domination of the drop.

Not only does the touch player have a passion for the drop but also he or she enjoys inflicting the torture a drop can deliver. I say this because the touch player knows that although a fit and agile player may retrieve most drops that retrieving this shot continuously is attributed to tiring an opponent more than any other shot in squash. In short, the touch player gracefully tortures his or her opponent to submission. But, I must admit that this notion holds second place for me. I cherish the moment when the gods imprinted the first idea of the drop in this player's heart and mind. The end product is then directly related to his or her desire.

Keep in mind that the best touch players are also designed a bit differently. Their limbs are longer. If you're a tall player, you could be an ideal candidate to develop the touch game.

But, whether you're an ideal candidate or not, remember it takes practice and flexibility to master the frontcourt. If you start now, you may at the very least develop a strong frontcourt game. And who knows? If you ever become a great touch player, you'll have what all players fear the most. And that's the torture you can inflict with a deadly drop in your arsenal.

#27

Squash players know that building both a sound offensive and defensive game takes time. The type of player you are is directly related in how a one of these styles will eventually dominate your game. All of this can be complicated. But, there is a certainty whether to play offensive or defensive immediately upon entering the court even for the very first time. The answer is obvious - it depends on who has the serve.

Every match begins with a serve. All should recognize the importance of being the server as well as the receiver. The serve in itself constitutes who is in a position of scoring a point and who must defend to prevent a point from happening. Understanding this makes the serve the greatest psychological element in the game of squash. Before serving an important point, take the time to briefly make eye contact with your opponent. It helps to make things sink in.

#28

Squash players know that building both a sound offensive and defensive game takes time. According to the type of player you are, is directly related to the fact in how a certain style will eventually dominate your game. All of this can be complicated. But, there is a certainty whether to play offensive or defensive immediately upon entering the court even for the very first time. The answer is obvious - it depends on who has the serve.

Every match begins with a serve. All should recognize the importance of being the server as well as the receiver. The serve in itself constitutes who must defend from a point being scored. And on the other hand, who has the opportunity to register a point.

Understanding this makes the serve the greatest psychological element in the game of squash.

29

Best and Worst Shots in Squash

1. There is only one bad shot and that's hitting it in the <u>MIDDLE OF THE COURT.</u>

2. Most important shots in every rally are the SERVE and SERVE RETURN.

3. Best Offensive Shot is the NICK. Best time is off the SERVE.

4. Best Defensive Shot is the LOB. Best time is a late retrieval of a front ct shot like a drop or Boast.

5. Most vulnerable part of the ct is the FRONT BACKHAND DROP AREA.

This is the best place to create openings as well as get in trouble.

6. Most secure part of the ct is the T.

7. Best shot to neutralize your opponent's attempt to control the rally are continuous BACKHAND DRIVES.

8. Best regrouping method to get back into a rally is again to fall back into BACKHAND DRIVES.

9. Best shot to practice to develop better timing is the VOLLEY.

10. First strategy to win at squash is to always STAY IN FRONT OF YOUR OPPONENT.

#30

Dissecting a Squash Court

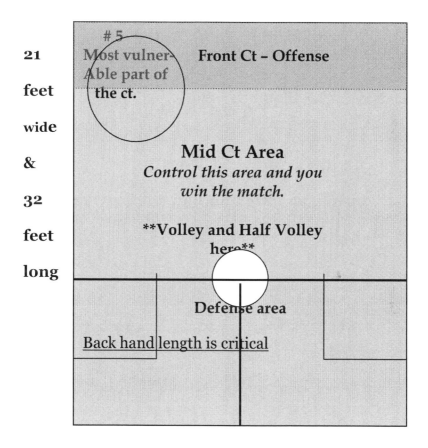

21

feet

wide

&

32

feet

long

5
Most vulner-
Able part of
the ct.

Front Ct – Offense

Mid Ct Area
*Control this area and you
win the match.*

****Volley and Half Volley
here****

Defense area

<u>Back hand length is critical</u>

* The T is the most secure part of the squash court.

*Controlling the T will use up less energy during points extending fitness for the duration of the match.

Front – Offense area

Mid – Both offense and defense (Control of this area wins a match)

Back court– Defense

Front ct – Best offensive shot is the DROP. The best defensive shot is the LOB.

Mid ct – Best place to control the rally and use up less energy in the process. Whoever controls this area usually wins the match. Best shots are the VOLLEY and HALFVOLLEY.

Back ct – Best defensive shot is the DRIVE. The backhand is more critical.

Best offensive shot is the BOAST.

Three points of contact in the three different areas of the ct for both the backhand and forehand account for the six points of the STAR DRILLS.

31

WHAT TO CONCENTRATE ON TO GET GOOD AT SQUASH

The basic shots in squash to develop are:

STRAIGHT DRIVE, CROSSCOURT, BOAST, DROP AND LOB

1. Understanding the nature of the game – Physical Chess.
2. Developing racquet skills – Drills and games – Develop arm and wrist strength.
3. Fitness – Games and Stars – first Arm and then Legs and Lungs.

4. ANTICIPATION – Knowing what your opponent will do.

5. Confidence – developing good concentration techniques – visualization - focusing.

6. Mental Toughness – all the above - NO FEAR over any course of time during competition.

7. In the final analysis, a player is only as good as his or her backhand.

8. The Opponent – Needs to be accessed. Check below.

9. Staying in front of your opponent in the match is the highest priority.

Offense and Defense

Offense can be measured by two things in squash:

1. The amount of Power in a shot to apply pressure.
2. Front ct. shots

Developing a strong wrist is first and foremost in squash.

The half volley shot develops wrist control quicker than any other shot.

Defense can be measured by:

1. The ability to keep the ball deep – good consistent length.

2. Slowing the pace down to help recovery.

**Having the serve means having the opportunity to score a point. Therefore, a simple tactic is to play more offensively when serving and more cautiously when playing a point not serving.

Things to watch for in the Opponent are:

1. Power
2. Level of control is measured in the Backhand.
3. Movement ability

Match Strategy

You are better than > Opponent

Offense > Defense

Make sure not to hit the same shots or your opponent will catch on.

Exploit the backhand to the fullest especially the front ct backhand area.

You are equally matched with your = Opponent

Offense = Defense

Biggest factor will be fitness. Bad LETS can disrupt play. Backhand drives should be hit more often than usual to set up the point.

You are clearly outmatched by your <

Opponent

Defense almost always. Go for the

Offensive Shot more often off the serve

return. Fitness is tested to the limit.

#32

I have been involved with squash for the last thirty-three years. In that time, not only have I learned much about the game, but I have also discovered goods ways to get a player to their highest potential. Once I realize a player's ability, I try to find out how coachable that player will be. Determining coachability is important.

It holds a critical key to the overall success of the player. There are many reasons why one player will improve faster than another. Mental toughness can determine this. It can come down to greater speed and agility. Cardiovascular fitness is also a definite factor. Better coordination can lead to smoother shot making ability and pull someone ahead. Sometimes one player will be more patient than another. A more intelligent game plan also plays a significant role. All in all, many components make up how one player will improve faster than another.

Regardless of how these components may overlap, an experienced coach can make a good assessment of a player's talent and future potential. A coach can determine, to a good degree, the physical ability and mental attitude of a player. A coach usually can establish how much experience a player has. And a coach can also determine strengths in technical ability. For squash it would be the ability to hit a shot well or how well a player can maintain correct footwork throughout a rally. Over time a coach will also come to know the personality traits within a player regarding desire, energy level and determination. All of this gives an accurate measure for how well a player will perform when the stage is set. Keep in mind that everything just mentioned is constantly fluctuating. With every illness, injury or significant time away from squash, things can weaken. A previously accessed way to improve a player's game may need to be revamped if there's a disruption in a training schedule. Any disruption will cause a player's game to disintegrate in some way. Fitness, court sense and confidence will all suffer. The usual outcome is a sub par performance and even a drop in ladder position.

In this type of situation where time is limited, players that can better implement a coach's advice will make up any lost ground faster. Not all players progress equally. Some definitely have a tougher time than others. Since time is always a critical factor throughout the season, players that don't bounce back begin to fall into a downward spiral. The end result is usually a below par season.

The ability for an athlete to implement any useful information by the coach quickly is the key. This is not a question of having an open mind or deeper concentration level or flipping a magic switch. It comes down to how well a player can add a change into his or her game. There is a method that works. Every action begins with a thought. The more a player thinks about an action, the more routine the action becomes. The more routine the action becomes, the less thought is needed. The action eventually becomes a permanent part of the player's game. Since this thinking pattern cannot be taught, every coach is thrilled when a player shows this ability. It reveals which player will make the most progress and strengthen the team.

Sometimes a change is needed in a player's game when time is not an issue. For example, a top ranked player on our team needed a new shot in his game. The shot needed is called the Nick. In this shot the ball is deflected off the front wall into the crack where the sidewall and floor meet on the opposite side of the court. If the ball is hit properly, the ball will hit the crack creating an instant winner. This is a common shot for higher ranked players.

This shot was definitely within the capability of this player yet he could not implement the shot. It was hard to get the shot to register in his head. A year later, after realizing that it was a common shot used by players against him, did he finally realize the potential weapon he could add to his game. He now hits the shot regularly but it took more than a year to have the shot implemented into his game plan. This was also a shot that another top ranked player needed to perform. He accepted the shot readily and learned to hit it within a month. He later became the team's MVP with the most wins during the season. A player with more experience also needed this shot. After three years of trying, he has not been able get it into his game. This is an example of adding a new shot for three very talented squash players. All had substantial experience, excellent athletic ability and solid mental toughness. All of them played well during some of the most intense times of the season. Yet, here the team's MVP would be described as the most coachable player because of his ability to add the nick to his game in the shortest amount of time.

In another example, two players on the women's team played every point with a high level of intensity – hitting the ball very hard throughout the longest rallies in every match. It was fun to watch and all the team players enjoyed the intense play. But, all this hard hitting sometimes got these two players out of position. They needed a good way to get back into the point and establish position in the middle of the courtI suggested that the players develop a good Lob. The lob is a high and slow shot capable of forcing an opponent deep into the back of the court. Since the lob is a slow high arching shot, it buys time to get back in position. Both women were experienced players with excellent ability and determination to win. I knew adding a lob to their game would have only positive results.

One of the players never developed a good lob. She had the talent and ability to execute the shot. She hit it well in practice. But, it was the nature of the shot that would not register in her head during a match. She played so hard all the time that hitting a slow lofting shot just did not click. The other player started out by really thinking about the shot. She had mentioned that she would get the shot in her game no matter what.

I told both players they needed to hit a lob occasionally at first and then pick up the frequency, as they got more comfortable with hitting it. The second player did just that. Today, she is the best lobber on the team. Consequently, she advises all the players on the team to develop the lob as part of their regular games. Later the team would elect her captain for the following season. Here, the second player would be the more coachable of the two. In both examples, the more coachable athlete was discovered after trying to implement a change. All the players I mentioned are strong in virtually every area that a coach could see. It was the implementation of a new shot or change in tactics that determined the more coachable player.

It is necessary to discover how coachable a player will be as soon as possible. It can reveal an accurate guideline to a player's learning curve. Some players can be so set in their ways that it is difficult to add any change. Nevertheless, through trial and error and with some diligence, a part of every player's game can be improved in one way or another.

I have found that coaching is not just sharing knowledge in a sport. It is also the ability to transfer that knowledge into a player's game. The coach's ability to communicate this is an important factor to ensure that the player understands what exactly needs to be done. Usually, if the coach and player agree to add a positive enhancement to the player's game, it then becomes a measure in the time it takes for the player to add that enhancement. I have used this measure of time to gauge the coachability of that player. I don't believe attitude is a factor because both agree to a certain change before making the effort.

Since both the coach and every player realize that it's vital to make changes to enhance improvement, both desire quick implementations so to move to the next area of concern. Usually both the player and coach agree that moving from one goal to the next as quickly as possible always produces the best results. But, if the player delays in any way, then moving from one goal to the next will stagger. Nevertheless, if the needed change is agreed upon in advance and if the coach has accessed the player's ability well, then it is assumed that the enhancement is within the player's capability to complete. Completion takes time. Cutting that time down as much as possible is always the primary goal. I have found that some players are more capable in this than others. This is no direct fault of the player. Some become extremely fixed in their ways. Finding ways to get players unfixed or convinced to make a change is not an easy task. The players who are less fixed and find ways to incorporate changes can also have fluctuations in their progress as well. Several enhancements may go well early on only to stagger later. Other times it is the enhancement itself that needs adjustment. Eventually both player and coach decide on something that works. Instead of trying to add the nick, it may make more sense to develop a more accurate drop. Instead of adding a lob to help positioning, it may be better to hit more crosscourts since clearing for the opponent is less critical. In both situations it still comes down to the player's ability to implement a needed change. The coach cannot help to measure how well a player implements his advice. The measure of progress always suggests either continuing down the same road or choosing another path that will work better for the player.

Throughout the season players watch one another and recognize who advances more in certain areas. One of the awards given in the squash program is the Most Improved Player Award. The players recognize who has made the most improvement and vote accordingly. After six seasons, I have come to realize that the recipient has always been the most coachable player on the team. He or she has implemented the most enhancements in the shortest span of time. The end result is a player who has improved the most regardless of circumstances.

In conclusion, I have found that a very talented player combined with a very experienced coach will not always create an even better player unless that player is fairly coachable. In the process, the more coachable player will undoubtedly build a stronger bond with the coach and get the most out of his or her game. Building this bond is certainly one of the best things that can happen in any sport let alone squash.

#33

Summary of SQUASH BASICS

1. Four things lead to playing good squash:

Always watch the ball make contact with the strings when hitting.

Always keep your racquet head up at all times.

Always recover to the middle of the court after hitting a shot.

Always watch your opponent hit the ball.

2. The two things to do in the
    beginning of every match:

First, hit the ball hard and get your
power established.

Second, make your first tough get as
soon as possible.

3. There are four simple rules in
    squash strategy:

First, stay on the T as much as possible
throughout the match.

Second, volley the ball whenever
possible.

Third, when you're in front of your
opponent, hit the ball short.

Fourth, when you're in back of your opponent, hit the ball deep.

4. All your shots should be accurate at the three designated points of contact.

> The first and most common point of contact is the <u>Ground Stroke</u> where the ball rises up to about knee level or higher.

> The second point of contact is the <u>half volley</u> or just off the floor.

And the third is the <u>volley</u> shot.

*What this means is that you can claim to have mastered a particular shot if you can execute it at these three points of contact with accuracy.

#34

There is a broad spectrum of concerns to develop a sound game of squash. A strong will to endure, fitness, strength, agility and patience are critical at the upper levels of play. In time all of these areas improve just by playing the game regularly. The fact of the matter is that squash needs these attributes if your plans are to excel at the sport. And how quickly you improve is determined by certain benchmarks.

First of all, keep in mind that your level of play is determined by how good your backhand is. If you have trouble returning high lob serves from the backhand corner, then it doesn't matter how good your drop is or how quickly you can move around the court. The deep backhand is the first obstacle every player needs to get through before thinking about extending a rally. Repeating specific shots in the form of drills will develop your patience as you perfect your accuracy. Some players need it more practice than others for certain shots. For example, some players master the deep backhand return more quickly than others. Regardless of where you stand, you need to get through these hurdles to get to your goal.

Once the deep backhand serve returns are accomplished with regularity then keeping the ball out of the middle must be addressed. With time as you improve your control; keeping the ball out of the middle will become less of a task. This will take time because you may be able to do this with certain players and not so well with others. Nevertheless, you must maintain the ability to keep the ball out of the middle most of the time in a match to develop any kind of good strategy in squash.

Let's say there comes a day when most of your shots no matter who you play are near the walls rather than the middle of the court. When this begins to happen, then hitting the ball deep or to good length is vital. Welcome to the beginnings of a winning strategy for squash. Still a bit confused about the next step. It's simple. After developing a good tight serve return; and keeping the ball out of the middle; and then hitting the ball to better length or (more often than not) to the back of the court, you ultimately begin to stay more in front of the court and command more time on the T. Remember in the end, the player that stays on the T, stays in front of his or her opponent and usually wins.

At this stage of the game you'll probably begin to play others that can keep the ball out of the middle and hit good length. Once this happens, you'll need to learn to dance. What I mean is that you'll now need to learn to hit a deep shot, move to the T and then back into a deep part of the court while your opponent is doing the same thing between exchanges. All of this should occur without bodily contact if possible. Some of the best footwork you'll ever need is not when executing shots but moving in and around your opponent without making contact and then getting in position to hit a good shot.

When anyone sees this, it looks like a kind of dance the two plays are engaged in. The higher the level, the smoother the two players dance around each other. It's great to watch and even better when you're in it with your opponent.

Most advanced players have this dance in the backcourt down to an art. It's the bases of good squash but it won't win matches. Players can keep this sort of thing up for long periods of time until someone decides to go short with the ball.

This is when the dance transforms from exchanges in the backcourt to a much more intense flurry of shots and movement in the frontcourt. Let's summarize.

After developing a good controlled return off the serve, and hitting the ball back deep and tight to the wall, controlling the T becomes pronounced. When we find someone else to play at the same level, a dance begins to ensue in the backcourt where we can move onto and off of the T with ease.

At this level, it becomes quickly apparent that sending the ball short is the only way to gain an advantage. Knowing when to do it is the key to how you think as an advanced squash player. How far you advance will be determined by your confidence, stamina and patience in this scenario.

Anyway, the next thing to accomplish is the ability to move one's opponent forward and back from time to time. This can be done with drops and boasts and quick intercepting shots in the air called volleys.

Boasts are shots deflected off any side way that makes the ball land in the frontcourt. Shots like this stretch your opponent forward breaking the momentum of having the rally secluded to the back of the court. It's the easiest way to move the rally to the front of the court. Executing the boast at the right time is gained only through trial and error and experience of common sense. When is that time? You'll know it in your gut.

The next area of concern once you attain the ability to play to whole court is to learn to cut the ball off by volleying. This is a critical shot in changing the pace of the ball and cutting your opponent's recovery time. This creates pressure and can exhaust your opponent. If enough control is acquired, a player can cut off shots using the volley and then send the ball into the back corners or even drop the ball into the front corners.

How creative you become is directly related to your positioning and confidence for volleying the ball. Your confidence is directly related to your ability. When you reach the uppermost realm in ability and confidence, you become a master who others watch and learn from. Discipline yourself from the start. As you get better, it's your frontcourt abilities that determine where you'll go in the squash rankings. Never let your guard down; keep your cool and the timing will come. I guarantee it.

#35

The mental game within squash is an obstacle at every level. Some pros are mentally tougher than others. They usually reside in the top rankings. In short, some players are mentally tough from the start while others it can become an overwhelming issue. Because of this, the mental game in squash is one of the biggest hurdles to overcome. How this part of your game develops, can only be determined by you. One thing is definite. It must be addressed because the mind can fluctuate throughout your progress in squash. Confidence today can quickly dissipate. I have found three things that can help.

First, we must add a repetition factor into your mindset. What I mean, is that, solo hitting builds confidence in your game. Whenever you feel the inclination to sharpen your squash wits, just jump on a court and hit the ball. Visualize, as you hit, where you're sweet spot is on the racquet. Feel it. Just getting the ball on the sweet spot continuously is the initial task. The solid feel in the sweet spot builds into mechanism of your stroke. Find it and stay on it throughout your hit. Any deviation in this could leave a tarnished spot on your mental armor.

Second, become so fit and fast that you realize you're practically unstoppable on the court. The best confidence next to hitting well is having a peak fitness level going into the next toughest match. Knowing this will make you more confident to stay on the court with anyone you play. Fitness is something that can't be overlooked at anytime especially when a major squash event is on the horizon. Without fitness, your mental game during competition will be weak from the start.

Finally, make sure to think about the big match as much as possible.

Visualize the intensity of the moment when you're in the fifth game serving at 10 all. Focus on the stress and anxiety of being in that situation and how you'll handle it.

Picture yourself double checking the score with the referee and walking back to the service box about to serve. Bounce the ball and see your sweat hit the floor next to your foot. Look over to your opponent for one last look to acknowledge the frenzy about to come. Realize this is a make or break moment in every sense of the scenario just envisioned. And make sure to do this as often as possible.

Remember that reflecting this kind of intensity over and over with purpose and imagination will get you ready for the real thing when it appears. And when it does, you'll be prepared. Simulating the experience in your mind over and over again will develop your mental toughness to the point of readiness and confidence to give you a distinct edge.

The difference between winning and losing usually comes down something you've done a bit differently to create an edge. This is just an example. During your squash progression you may discover things that work better for you. Whichever paths you take, always remember - play to win!

Manufactured by Amazon.ca
Bolton, ON

14296723R00141